MOTHER MUSE QUINTET

Naveen Kishore

MOTHER MUSE QUINTET

SPEAKING TIGER

SPEAKING TIGER BOOKS LLP
125-A, Ground Floor, Shahpur Jat, New Delhi 110 049

The poems on pages 3, 6–7, 10–12, 13–15, 16 and 20 were first published in *Another Chicago Magazine* (15 April 2021; anotherchicagomagazine.net)

This edition first published by Speaking Tiger, 2023

ISBN : 978-93-5447-496-5

eISBN: 978-93-5447-482-8

10 9 8 7 6 5 4 3 2

Typeset in Dante MT by Sunandini Banerjee, Seagull Books
Printed at Chaman Enterprises, New Delhi

CONTENTS

MOTHER MUSE I

She carried crumbs. Every single morning. The smell of bread. Every single morning. For as long as I can remember. For as long as she can remember. She never forgot to scatter the crumbs. In every conversation. Like puzzles. Or clues. To help her find her way home. Later. Much later. When the mist from over there would begin to rise. Stretch out. Start to take charge. Like the inevitable damp. Cling to things. In and around her. Then, those scattered clues. Like markers in a treasure hunt. Those planted hints. They were the advance guard. In a war that would surely take place. But in her innocence she had failed. To realize. That the first casualty would be the power lines. Short-circuited. The enemy would cut off her ability to recognize. To recall her masterplan. To recognize the very signs she had so diligently left in place. Now they were part of a geography lesson. A map of an alien landscape. Of her own making.

The sun.
In a boat. Being ferried
to the other side. Bearing light.
Bearing Light.

Coiled
deep in head made silence
this snake out of breath
having run itself into the ground
faltering just when it mattered
mattered most to whom
unable to keep time stopwatch awry
bean counters in a humid haze
dazed as they meander along byways
like conversations deep in throats too full
of yesterday's babel
anxious afraid fearful
so much happens in the beat that beat
beat beats a heartbeat that splitting of a
second into more seconds
or would that be thirds fourths fifths
the smashing crumbling into atoms
these fragments of measured time
endlessly breaking
pick up the scatter lying in the
rubble rising remnants over
what only the shadows can know
as they announce their arrival
like waves dashing their selves
into rocks armed to the
teeth laughing
over what

Picture this. The child of two. Three and four. Dodging her legs. Adept. Agile. Adroit. Hiding between the folds of her sari. Camouflaged against the 'enemy'. All the adults out there. Except her. No. Never her. Shyness as curse? Or protection? In my mind, the sari she wore is always a pale pink. Almost ivory. And a chiffon. Let us give her a name, shall we? Mother.

Then it fades.

Picture this. The child of nine. A park somewhere. A cricket match. The first bloodied nose. Wasn't the ball that did it. Wasn't the friends either. The details are blurred. The memory-frames begin to jump. Something to do with a dog. A man throwing a stone at a dog. The dog in pain. Bleeding from one eye. Anger. White and blazing. I run headlong at the attacker with all the strength of a niner-in-rage—and that's all I remember. Timeout. The film slices its sprockets. Pool of black and white at my feet. Silent. I remember telling my mother that I had walked into Gregory's wrought-iron bedstead.

Picture this. A room somewhere. Old. Haunted by thoughts I haven't visited since childhood. An entire lexicon of memories concealed behind the peeling paintwork. As I scrape the paint off, a cascade of words pitter-patter onto the floor. The work of children hiding their true feelings from adults. Garbled sentences. Out of sequence. Ideas that once held promise. Now gone. Slowly, I drown in the rising tide of language. Odd, that my mother and I had so much we said to each other.

There's more. You walk through the door. Into a fog. The grey of a winter morning making its home on your side of the threshold. You wander. Feel the damp on your arms. The air is thick with songs that caress your senses. You slowly drift off to sleep on her lap. Five years old and already you can tell the difference between Kishore Kumar and Manna Dey. It will take a while before I understand the concept of 'playback singing'.

It is the seamlessness of remembering that amazes me. Memories. Yours and mine. The ones you enthralled me with on our long walks. And much later, my retelling of the 'tales' you told me. 'Making up' what had slipped past me. I gave them the happy endings you never had. There were times when you took me by the hand and introduced me to your father. A grandfather who'd died years before I was born. But a grandfather I knew so intimately because of you. He would read to me from screenplays he had freshly baked. Enacting each of the parts. I could almost see him before me. Many years later, you would come home from your Friday matinee and enact the film of the week. Playing twenty different parts. Seamlessly.

You gifted me my memory.
We did not know then
that one day you would lose yours.

persuade breath stop pull back hands cajole plead clock turn time stop time pause time take stock halt time whatever it is that clocks do to *bring back that one moment* slam shut the door on fingers made numb so I may feel pain grieve a little longer distract time step back move sideways and forward anything confuse time images a childhood spent in patches of sunlight gathering pebbles while adults hatch plans of shooting photos on Agfas from another time to *bring back that one moment* capture trap still time remind rewind playback payback time signs of growing up crisscross a landscape moving in the opposite direction what could we do what could we do to take stock halt time whatever it is that clocks do to *bring back that one single moment* of sunlight as you stand aslant the shadows counting hours spit on stones and polish them with your seven-year-old hands filling pockets as many as you can gather weigh down time from another time cajole plead clock turn stop time grieve stay still as the shadows move the hands of the clock plead pause stop distract step back move sideways and upwards images of an adulthood you left behind *bring back that one moment this one time*

She was turning seventy-five. She didn't see it as something special. The clear smile hadn't begun to lose its warmth, even as the mist had begun to appear at the fringes of her universe. Shuffling along the walls. Trying to find a crevice through which to creep in. Take up residence. Entice the fog to follow. I remember buying her so many presents. There were the salwar and kameez sets. Three of them. With contrasting or matching dupattas in her favourite dizzy lizzie fabric or very fine cotton. Weightless. Almost as if the haze that would appear before her eyes was making a peace offering—a bouquet of printed flowers—this one last time. There were the lemon-yellow roses she adored. A dozen of them. And a ceramic vase. Deep blue. Its edges tinged with gold. A watch with a thin leather strap. Her metal one had begun to bother her. Steel grey. A white dial with large digits that glowed in the dark. A silver picture frame with a colour photograph of her and Dad from some years ago, taken at the Botanical Gardens. A pair of blue slippers to wear around the house. A spectacle case that shut with a sharp magnetic click. Olive green. With pale yellow flowers. And a wall mirror. Around twenty-four inches in length and eighteen inches in width, with a dark-brown three-inch wooden frame inlaid with flowers in burnished gold. Perhaps I had noticed that she had no dressing table in front of which to comb her hair.

Later. In the afternoon. For tea. There would be cake. Eggless. Chocolate.

She opened each gift with care. She belonged to a generation that liked saving the wrapping paper. She folded each sheet carefully. Made appropriately grateful noises over each object and made me feel that I had chosen well. But there was an air of detachment that manifested itself without in any way lessening the warmth. I sensed it but it didn't ring any alarm bells. Nor did I feel she was thanking me because that is what one did on such occasions. That wasn't her way at all. Only when she arrived at the large mirror did she falter and solicit my assistance in opening it. I did. And held it for her to admire. Holding it in front of her face as she sat in her sofa chair.

She looked up at me. Not at the mirror. At me. Her eyes serious. Quiet. Not saying anything. Then with what seemed for the first time an effort she smiled. Thanked me. And started to talk. About I am not sure what. But no longer about the gifts.

I arranged to put up a nail at her eye level and hung the mirror. On the wall that faced her bed. Between the door to her room and her bathroom. Ease of convenience.

Strangely enough. I never saw her using it. She didn't avoid it but she never looked into it. Just continued to comb her hair in the small bathroom mirror for the rest of the years she was with us.

Later of course it wouldn't matter. Her gaze had already turned inward. Not inward looking. Or seeing. Or meditative. Just. Inward.

The mirror is still there. On the nail. On the wall. In the room we still think of as hers.

Her father decided to name her Prem. 'It means love,' he said. Later he would call her Prema-ji. The 'ji' was a term of respect reserved for older folk. But he liked using it for her. Signalling his love and respect for the little girl who would soon start to live up to her name.

They were comrades from the time she was four. Sharing secrets. And laughter. She was the apple of his eye. The star he followed around their rather large house, with all its twists and turns. Its steps and courtyards full of whistling summer winds. Its terraces that invited the winter sky into the warmth. And the well at the far end of the courtyard, with its braided rope of many colours and tiny bells. Every time father and daughter lowered the bucket for water, a million tinkling chimes would fill the air. As if all the temples in the world had decided to ring their bells at once.

He delighted in capturing her every waking moment on his 16-mm camera. She didn't mind. She didn't pose. She wasn't playing for the camera—she was just playing. The happy child she was. Full of the love of life. And he, proud father, doted. Adored. He was many things to her. Her horse. Her elephant. Her bear who danced to her tiny drum. Their time together was made up of playing hide and seek; flying kites; and storytelling. They would read. She from the Urdu fairy tales that were doing the rounds in the Lahore of the thirties. And he from the screenplays he penned for a living. For the silent films.

I never met him. He had moved on before I was born. He must have known that his beloved land would soon tear itself into two. Not wanting to see that happen, he simply walked away. To the other side. Leaving her behind. To finish his incomplete stories.

I heard those stories from her. His. Theirs. The family's. The life before. And after Partition. She had a knack for narrating the worst possible inhumanity known to man in such a matter-of-fact style, you felt that nothing could turn her into a bitter person. This was what people did to each other. One had to make the best of it. Survive. With dignity. Pick up the pieces. Rebuild. She had put their initial play to good use. And become a master story-teller. Not just at bedtime to us youngsters but also at any time of the day. She didn't describe scenes. She lived them. Intuitively. Conjuring up an entire scenario before my amazed eyes. Complete with sound effects and unheard music. My ears hanging on to every nuance and tone of voice as she played the various parts. The characters coming alive. I would often reach across and touch them. Become a part of their life. And tale. It was a gift she had inherited. From him.

I decided to call her by her name. Prem. With a ji. So Prem-ji. The loved one. I grew up listening to all her family, sisters, her mother, her aunts calling her Prema. So before I could graduate in earnest to Ma, it was Prem. And it stuck. Other people found it strange. Even odd that a young person would call his mother by her first name. For me it was natural. And special.

And she? She was generous enough to let me do this.

For the rest of our lives together.

There were days when she didn't remember. Failing to realize something was amiss yet knowing something was not quite right. Hesitation. A parallel tango of knowledge and its lack. It was a fog that came unannounced. Crept in from under the door. Like this morning. The parting of last night's curtains. Letting in the light. Bright. The gold of the tea. In the porcelain cup. The one with the wide mouth. Light. Glinting off the silver service. Into her eyes. The sparkle anticipating a day. Signs of beginning afresh. Like a promise. Then the walk. To the mirror. Anticipation. The smiling at an image. Of oneself. Familiarity turning to despair. In a single particular moment. Of knowing. Not knowing. The eyes staring. At the rising fog. Unable to register. The image in the mirror. A face that stared back. But failed to see. Through the fog. Her face. No longer her own. The shutters were beginning to descend. The descent into the well. Always the descent. Each time. But never the same well.

Build me a self. She pleaded. A whole one? I asked. One I may call my own. Self. Again. She said. I looked at her. Swiftly. Almost surreptitiously. My gaze. First taking in the dignity. The earnestness. Hers. And of the request. The controlled undertone. Not quite panic. Yet. And trust. The faith. That I could. And would. Help rebuild. Not just her self. But also her sense of being. Hers. No room for doubt. Or error. Not in her mind. Her mind that had known nothing. A will. So strong. And purpose. Now a tremor. Her mind. A sustained flicker. Twitching. In hesitation. Her own. The light squeezed out. The fog rolling in. The curtain going up. The play is the thing, she said. Just like that. Out of the blue. No longer able to perform. The lines no longer consuming her. You forget lines. Sometimes. She added. Quietly. Like the back of your hand. You no longer recognize. As your own. And life. The rest of your life. Now no longer familiar. Yes, you forget the streets. In particular. The street you live on. The remembering. Forgotten. Not gradually. But a sharp click. And a lingering aftertaste. From the life before. The night before. Or the morning after.

Preferring the safety of the wings. The shades at the end of the slope. Steep. The hill. The street. My mother. Boldly heading out. Towards the shadows. Like tumble-weed, hurtling. Downwards and up. At her.

Hear that
gust of wind
sharp

a bolt snapped shut

the tear slid down
the cheek made slope
a solitary descent

elsewhere

a half-shut window
its hinges thirsting
for oil

rattling
in the wind
a winter

long gone come
to solicit death
no longer

at arms' length

its shadow growing
climbing up

swallowing the wall
like ivy

devouring everything

the storm in rage
grinding itself
to a halt

its foot jammed
in the door

stillness ruptured
stillness

I held her in my hands. Her once-cold body. Now warm. Hot even. Like a rising fever. Scalding my hands. Wanting something to remember her by. I squeezed my hands shut. Tight. Like my eyes. Till the tears came. Then I opened the hand full of ash. Slowly bent down. At the edge of the water. And let go. Giving what remained of her. Up. Into the care of the river. Watched her bob up and down. Make her way. Deftly sidestepping all the other remains. Charting her own course. Gone. All that remained was the gift. The scar. On the palms of my hands.

warm dark safe
shadow secure
this
shelter

open the shell
my palms have formed
as I stepped ginger-footed
out
out from the crevices
of my hand straighten
my cramped legs
and elbows
smoothen
the creases give
my self a good
shake head to the left head to the right ease
the neck muscles

look at the cave I had decided to leave
my face not betraying any emotion none
whatsoever

walked into the sunlight
failing to succumb
even once
to the temptation of looking back

leaving behind the child
            in the care of shadows
that were trained

in the art of child-rearing

She looked at him like you would into a mirror stepping all over her scattered self like you would look at the end of a night that had begun in a vague sort of manner like nights sometimes do dishevelled she looked at him like you would reflect back at a self once full of self seeing her beginning to blur like you would at the end of the night that had started then scattered like nights sometimes do disperse fan out you would say would you not their contours vague their minds edgy unsure not quite made up they could go on and on their selves lengthening unsteady of feet you would say think ponder the haze leaking from their eyes would slowly begin to dilate on a night like the one this is turning out to be as she looked at the mirror and as the silver once firm hard resolute turned to water its waves resembling the sea at high tide as if inviting her to drown

shapeless
time
crumbling

the sun
hiding itself in the trees

horizons twisted knotted
attempting to win
a tug of war

ageing in silence
the ground
the earth shifts

while
the haze around my eyes
sways in hesitation

She imagined rather she said these words imagine then stopped to pause for effect as predicted as I had assumed to predict listening to this voice risen from the long-locked cellar she had inhabited in her imagination or in the life she had chosen not chosen to dis inhabit but again I assume while she lengthens the pause of the imagine as if she too had just found after some difficulty and soul-searching her voice imagine finding yourself adrift on a sea under an open sky with only the sounds of the sea lapping your ears in an almost lullaby imagine then my surprise as I struggle to keep up with the route trajectory of this wandering for I had expected presumed assumed that the imagination would move elsewhere not sure where but certainly not this this sky from the cellar dream seemed what a bit unreal but then was that not the intent of the actor to surprise imagine then the unpredictability of belief when the knife now twisted into a pliant flesh would find the joy it had sought of completely overpowering the enemy the listener who knew or thought so anyway so yes imagine then the lullaby the lament the unwillingness to follow this dreaming under a sky on a mattress that knew no boundaries afloat healing waiting for a storm that may yet arrive and yet to presume assume imagine that you understand the ways of the wind the lashings and the lacerations of the storm would be foolish foolhardy even would it not

hidden twice   hidden
among pages made brittle
                    poems that reside
like   flowers
rusted
with age
who
placed them there?

stem cutshort
unable
to draw blood
from rosepetals
blunt thorn

leafslicing
through the air
beneath my feet
the debris
of fallenflowers

clutching
a flower drowning
in ink
I dream of
spread-eagled lilies

the dream ploughing its way
through the heat
as fields of mustard
catch fire
the fragrance of burning leaves

the flowers turn to rust
the river
in all its holiness
drowns
in a fistful of ash

talk to me won't you
wind on a breathless day
don't just lie
whitefaced
upon the leaves

let me sleep
then this long sleep
sleep at length this sleep and
awaken
among the white flowers

do you shiver
are you cold
or are you come alive
blasted wind
to my touch

do not awaken me now
now that I am forever asleep
here among the leaves
that the flowers in their hurry to flee
left behind

a different wind not one I knew or recognized or had learnt to be comfortable with no a new wind not necessarily an unpleasant or difficult one just unfamiliar not easy to pin down perhaps yes even a little aloof not cold nor arrogant or with any hint of malice and yet with an air of sharpness akin to an aura of briskness suggesting hinting wanting to get down to the work at hand as it were for there was a lot to be done but not impatient or irritable so yes with an understanding awareness with a tinge of courtesy this wind and one that dare I conjecture one that gave the impression of being reasonably well bred both in the way it behaved and looked and most certainly a well-read wind one that seemed to be educated I am simply guessing I am simply sensing something in the air nothing definitive after all it is all so intangible this seemingly sense-driven feeling about something neither solid nor firm an air that purports to be different an air that has within it a sense of both difference and indifference and were we to extend the word play a bit one could go on to suggest that the visibly more solid player in this game would be the me of my self who senses strongly the difference in the air around me that leads me to comment on the difference in the quality of the wind also around me and the wind itself that is completely and utterly incapable of anything other than a simple and airy indifference in the face of all my senses and sensations

dark light   sometimes
unafraid
fearless
not always   sometimes
the voices
emerge
hard to decipher
not sure   why
I know she's gone

why would I want to believe this?

I see
the dream walking around
the house   sitting too
my mother
had she lived
would have had to learn
to walk
all over again
on legs that no longer   belonged
but that's another story

people die
mothers
fathers too

I know
this
for a fact
naked light
I let them cut off her leg
in an effort to ease her pain.

what else was there to do?

The fog can be a welcoming place but we don't know that till we step into the fog its white walls seem to recede and come at you at the same time like milk deprived of gravity floating a slow-motion photograph the waves rising gathering momentum before dancing all over you as you go down the hole hurtling through and down and down till you sprawl crumple somersault tumble into and then without so much as a breath the fog topsy-turvies your body into a balletic curve and lends your feet the wings of angels so you may fly or pirouette at the same time as it makes sure the blindfold you wear in sympathy is in place and not in danger of slipping off for how else would you ever begin to sense to fathom what it must have been like for her as she without legs to stand on and definitely devoid of the wings she never knew were hers for her fog and this fog I write about are different are they not for they must be. They. Must. Be.

They must have been different hers and mine for her not to sense that the muscles she put into motion when she looked at me were fashioning themselves into a smile only she no longer had words to describe the emotion that may have crept across her face had she remembered to enact it having forgotten even those lines the ones with which she had spread her affections in days when her mind did remember did understand did connect or that her smile had been stolen of its warmth and she had not reported the theft not known how to not known who to not known. What else.

She steps knowingly unknowingly into a fog waiting for her shadow to catch up and does not notice that she no longer has words to cajole persuade beseech and nor does her shadowy self to recover what is now lost for them both their past adrift its long iron chain gathering rust perhaps the two do not even have a name for this heartbreaking namelessness that they watch not sure whether to jump in or struggle with this inexplicable embrace of white as they watch themselves slip. Slip. Slip away.

Her face no longer the home I came back to the eyes no longer the sparkle that dazzled and amused and entertained us all with countless stories made up on the run to hold our attention now hers was slowly losing its anchor its moorings its hold removing itself from us our world the one she had helped create build nurture a world that would soon recede from her like the tide that forgets ebb and flow and simply gives up breathing crashing against the rocks for the last time and losing itself into foam. Foam like. This. Fog.

inheriting the fog speech lost words blindfolded racing
round bends curves soundlessly on perfectly controlled
breath scattering an army of alphabets rotten putrid sullen
falling over the edge into their own silence

brick by brick the babble
demolished

Grey mumblings as if lost the clouds grey hesitant as if holding their breath grey walls shifting imperceptibly as if lost in a trance almost out of breath spinning letting go their arms legs hands stretching upwards as if where the head once attached now as if floating almost swallowed engulfed by grey walls shifting as if unable to hold as grey mumblings grow louder as if in spate the river grey waves lending muscle lending shoulder lending voice rising as if about to burst banks bending curving its grey waters spilling over as if about to first drown itself then the skies as if

Far gone and silver-haired and yet vain enough to stare at the mirror as I carefully first oiled then combed her hair with equal parts sunshine and fading hope trying not to look too hard into the vacant eyes staring back at me in what appeared to be a silent thank you.

How frail she is I remember thinking.

I would sit in the silence of her thought in the room alongside mine. Rehearsing. A parallel performance. As she sat. Her lengthening shadow. A stranger to us both. Her stillness sinking into the twilight. The bucket now rusted is lowered into the well. At the end of the courtyard. The rope is threadbare. It crashes into the stone walls. Then it disappears into the water. Her mother and her mother's mother before her. Had been here. Once. In this state of absolute stillness. They too had looked out from within a thoughtful silence. In preparation. Observed their shadows. Stretching into blindness. Crashing into the wall at the far end of a room. The room itself. Carefully prepared. Cleansed of all thought. Made bare. And still. Like a stage that had been set. Precisely for this purpose.

By now only the white. Like a cloak discarded by a hurriedly departing angel. Rising swirl of tender forgetfulness. The fog. White. Leaking from the corners of her eyes. Light tentative. Her once all-seeing eyes now grasping at whispers. From across a bridge creaking. With the weight of memory. I lean forward.

My confusion a bundle of unravelling string. Becoming longer and longer. For there is no flicker. None. Here gaze. There. Unsteady. Unable to locate the fear. Lurking in mine. Unconcealed. No sign then. Or now. Of having heard.

That we will no longer walk Together That her leg now rotted will no longer Bear her weight That the pain will only end On losing the leg That it would need to go Go from above the knee So on And So forth.

No sign. Of having heard. Then or Now.

Turning abruptly away from the white I stumble out. Into the fog.

Unable.
just waiting

the light

plays		her skin

lies	across a bed

that

waits

scalded

an avenging sun

the	light

in the mirror

overflows

MOTHER MUSE II

seeking a particular death large-hearted
half-hearted sauntering
like taking one's shadow for a walk
by the river

At the edge at the edge of the echo then she said just above the precipice you know the one I mean the precipice near the rim do you know it the rim twice gilded its circles gilt-edged rings one above the other like suspended halos that an angel left behind attempting to meet as they hovered glowing in perfect symmetry lit by what remained of the trailing light as the sun departed as it sank helplessly it is said into sound that lay at the edge of the echo in all its purity characterized by the clarity of its radiating waves meet me there she said again almost in a whisper a whisper made melody made echo at its edge just above the precipice that looked down at the abyss from over the rim a rim no longer lit by the sun that had meanwhile set without ceremony in silence without a whisper or sound of any kind.

Clear then your throat. She said. Sing. She said. Sing the end of the world to me.

Come back
to this shadow
now swept under light
room after room
of memories stacked
from floor to ceiling
testimonies
held together by pieces
of mismatched string

the taste
of a tongue   coated with
dry rust
          the smell   of a sudden
departure
like the trapped escaping of breath
loud as the ocean
between the ears
shells   seeking refuge
from a sea   hell-bent
on expelling them

what is the colour of leave-taking?

even as I
prepared to light
the sticks of incense
in the room you deserted
choosing instead
the smell of the earth
damp inside
deeper earth
you who had little choice
you said
but to give in
to this
this thing
growing
inside death's body

shrunk to half your size
the worms their fancy
taking wing
already
beginning
a journey

the long pause slices at the edge of reason overflows like
the fog from a machine unhinged from its fan-shaped
exterior the grief waiting to be cradled grows as it tries to
count the number of years an abacus of remembrance
playing memory games and losing

rust twilight the ground beneath your feet trampled by
blind mourners their voices rise and ebb throats parched
the rain seeks shelter your denial an inexplicable testimony
of reason at the edge of grief failing to remember its
own beginning as you overthrow the queen in one single
flourish and smile check

thought congealed only the blood remains trapped
between the thumb and the forefinger unsure whether
the next breath will be its last as the flies from a haze-filled
life happen to chance by wondering if it is too late to feast
upon the overflowing grief at the edge of reason

only the light knows its shadow and remains deathly still

changed *now*
changed
everything different
even
the dreams
changed *now*
waking up
middle of the night
now changed
now
the storms stalk
the wind *now*
the light
now different
changed
everything *now*
hesitant unsure changed
now the stillness
seeking a refuge
from
an unchanged darkness
now

MOTHER MUSE III

you could have if you wanted to interrupted the silence

as it sliced through the landscape

There are many ways a child will learn its mother's tongue. Spoken from a far-off place while the protective cocoon of the womb holds it secure but allows it to listen. Every murmur. Every whisper. Finds its way to the child's heart.

Before it begins to speak.

I first learnt the language my mother spoke while I slept in her lap. In Kashmir. The first words I heard were not spoken. But sung. I heard songs. As murmurs. As whispers. As lullabies. As language that soothes. And invites the welcoming night to a child's tired eyes. So that they may close and rest. These were my night sounds. Sounds that lulled me to sleep.

The morning sounds were different. Their timbre more deep. They were songs that flowed effortlessly from my father's throat. He sang while he dressed for work. The popular hits of the time. Kundan Lal Saigal's ghazals; C. H. Atma; Talat; Suraiya, Noor Jahan . . . the songs that heroes and heroines of the black-and-white era sang to each other, expressing love and anger and happiness and sorrow and despair and heartache and joy and devotion and war and famine birth and death. He seemed to know them all.

Later. The filmfolk from Bombay discovered Kashmir. My father as assistant manager and host at the Oberoi Palace would invite the Kishore Kumars, the Talats, the Nargises and Sunil Dutts, the Padmini and Ragini sisters, the Raj Kapoors, the Simis to his humble quarters at the foot of the hill and just above the hotel's rooms and vast lawns. My mother's tomato pulao and kheer and gajar ka halwa was loved by the visiting stars who relaxed after a hard day's shoot, happy to unwind and make themselves at home. Sitting on our mats and eating from our thalis. The evenings would begin and end in song. Singing soirees at home.

Sleeping in her lap. Comfortable. Secure. Drifting back to the memories of a time before I was born. I would listen from afar even as I fell into deep sleep.

Years later I would remember the ghazals and the songs. I would hum the tunes. Later. Much later, I would begin to speak Hindi and Punjabi and bits of Urdu.

Even later, the nuns of St Presentation Convent would take me into their charge and teach me a whole new language.

English.

Unravelled
the scream lay
down
among the lilies
facedown

You could
if you thought
you could climb
the tree and shake it *hacksaws and blades as long*
as the night
till the mangoes
dropped on the street *slice cut-open pulp*
then you could if
you thought you should
simply gather the mangoes
that dropped from the tree *branches*
their hands blistered
you could *you could*
stop the screaming

They don't make beds like that any more. So high that a seven-year-old would need a stool or at least a helping shove to get on them. Wide and long. Teak from Burma. Slatted underbelly. What else? Lot of room underneath for playing 'house-house'. I would spend hours under them. With my books, a table lamp, pillows, a bed sheet and my grandmother's *shakarparas* for company. Sometimes, I would fall asleep there but then wake up in my own bed in the room down the corridor. At other times, I would be forgotten for hours on end. Even days. Or so I'd like to believe. On one such day, all the play would leave my life forever.

All I have is this image. A photograph as old as the memory it has sworn to secrecy. For forty-nine years. Vertical. Unusually elongated. Frayed. Tinted or bleached. Pinkish sepia for two-thirds of its length and urine stained for the rest. The woman in the picture is standing still. Stillness within the stillness of the photograph. A stillness born of shame. And defiance. The salwar and kameez that my mother is wearing in the memory are wet. Drenched. Not by rain or by water. But by dark stains that mimic the animated frames of a forest fire. Without beginning and showing no signs of end. The face, lowered and tilted to the left, hand-smeared with what looks like paint. Not one layer, many. The eyes, shut. Long hair, streaked as if by tar, half-covered by a dupatta. Equally tarred. Arms folded across her breasts. The right hand clutching the top of the left shoulder. The left holding up the right elbow.

Fearing that the pack of braying hyenas would break down his door, my father's elder brother, my own uncle, in whose care my father had left us, sacrificed her that day to the Holi revellers.

And I?

All I have is this photograph.

This one has water too. Or, rather, ice. Large quantities of it. In slabs. Here too she gets sacrificed. Almost.

Not a photograph. A black-and-white film. A tilting upwards of the camera behind the eyelids. Slow movement. Quiet. Verging on the imperceptible. So as not to disturb the cataract.

Dawn fights to conceal the fading night. Or the grey of a successful monsoon. The light from the large window on the right is vintage morgue. The silence in the room is in deference to the large slabs of ice on which lies this young woman. Pale. White. Beautiful in sleep. As she was in waking. Her waking, an already-fading memory. The four-year-old feels only the chill of her bed from his corner near the door. He is not allowed to go near her.

In his dream, he has crept under the safety of the bed. Images of games yet to be played in the sanctuary of this home ricochet inside his head. In his nightmare, the cold floodwaters caused by the melting of the ice are threatening to drown him. This is a dream that repeats itself. Image. Dream. Nightmare. Each time, it is the pale lifeless hand of his mother that reaches into the whirlpool and pulls him out.

By her side, near the head, caught in the same grey of the early-morning morgue light sits my father. It is he who has carved this bed of ice to calm the raging mercury that refuses to climb down from the ledge of the 108th floor. Two days of beseeching. Every moment a lifetime. He is trying to breathe life into what the doctors have pronounced dead.

Somewhere in the corner of my head where I crouch or from under the bed where I drown is a hand-operated sewing machine being furiously being spun by my grandmother. Repetitive tumbril. *Mar gayee to kya hua? Aur le ayenge.*

My helplessness was no match for his resolve. He won.

She lived.

she lay there. bleeding a red that impregnated the white cotton sari from the front. on the bed. on her side. one quivering hand clasping another. asleep or meditating. who could tell. i thought of ink as it spreads on blotting paper. slowly moving. forward and sideways. the folds of the sari doubling as small pouches. getting heavier with the weight of the advancing liquid. drop by drop. on the sheet. then the floor. red on red. like lava.

something inside her had burst.

radhasoami . . . radhasoami . . . radhasoamiradhasoamiradha-soami . . . radhasoami . . . an incessant chant that came from the corner of the room in which she lay for two years. waiting to go. bedsored and mired in her own mess. her daughter-in-law, my mother, would have to clean her. not once. nor twice. but twelve to fourteen times a day. I was her apprentice. often having to swallow the vomit welling up inside me. all my finickyness forgotten. or suppressed. sometimes the rancid liquid would seep through the cotton wad and wrap itself around my fingers. i too had learnt to pray to her god. about death. hers. why didn't she die and end our misery. and her own. but her god, oblivious as she was, seemed to prefer waiting. waiting for her to go on her own. without help. and yet, she was dead for everyone except my mother. and me.

death as relief.

now there is him. her son. my father. and there is the chant. *radhasoami . . . radhasoami . . . radhasoamiradha-soamiradhasoami . . . radhasoami . . .* a ghostly reincarnation in a body that has slowly isolated itself from friends and loved ones. a life in retreat. from what? or in retaliation. against what? dead by most standards. certainly not missed. and my mother? she is still cleaning sores from a different bed. her own. fifty-five years of inching towards her own death. and his. only he seems to have got there before her. yet he's here. miserable by his own making. misery for her of his making. and hers. bound together and waiting to leave.

something inside him had burst.
something inside me has burst.
burstburstburstburstburst.

I recall conversations. with him. with her.
but never together.

night
nightlong night
long shadows
sunlit
a solitary echo
seeks refuge
among the crows
blinded
eyes
dreaming
a pilgrimage

inside
my home
a reluctant
storm
anticipates
its whispered end

the smell of rust
lying   in wait
in that particular   corner
of the room
full
of interrupted dreams
naked footsteps pacing
their own babel

or is it
?

unlike
the sum of all my autumns

hard to say   or comment
when you find you are   unable
to wrench yourself   out
of the dream

it isn't
as if   you wish   to see the dream
through to the end

          is it
          ?

Do not remind me
I know
I know
how close she is
rank foul silent persistence
nor may I escape her
shadow in the dark nor
be lulled by her song
lullabies glorifying a sleep
purposeless
the dangling of promises
of an afterlife
flowered by spring
promises I know
I know
to be untrue

the words tainted sullied even from use abuse excessive
battered bruised unable to heal this wounded sky

scarred

caress the white of the wall hands grazing as they hugged
the contours the bumping over cracks the odd precipice
the hills of peeling paint an occasional avalanche of
plaster come undone at the curves as

the night meandered not out of leisure but a forced
restlessness controlled by an urge to stretch itself longer
than its allotted time

lingering

just

bare
un inhabited
haunted damp seeking
refuge

seeping
through cracks in the
fog
not quite habitat

not yet

Harsh beam of white like light razor edge unleashed whip lashed across skin made sky red sun in tatters drilling itself into a tunnel relentless narrow shaft of pain unburdened unwept swept under thick dust leaves crusted congealed unable to move limb nor muscle twisted arms legs shoulders a tangle of flesh as the knife from the surgeon's toolbox cut precisely from the navel to the core of her being made nothing unuttered scream lodged deep in throat as the mouth formed over knuckles revealing smashed bone crushed between teeth the sound dying unwed eyes closing to reveal undreamt dreams seeking a burial ground to rest in unsolicited uninvited.

MOTHER MUSE IV

A Meditation on Time Passing

abandoned

by day

        by night

        breath

        out of breath

wilt time

        wander

        light

fall

off the edge   of the page

        drown time

inherit words

soaked

in solitude

time silenced memories

her

room

anchored

in shadow

sunlight from another day

time marooned

her

absence

imprisoned as if

by what else

time

green leaf

spiral

to your death

afterthought

a god in a hurry

a childhood orphaned

by haze

by daylight

dulled

time

a time

before time strayed

into the hands

of a malicious god

make pale my words

yellow light

of winter

slice the leaves

the trees

wind-chilled

a face

no longer warm

wrinkled around

eyes

that once were

witness

resist sun

words late

for the revolution

their arrival

a hurried departure

dig

hole

bury shadow

any shadow

no room for daylight

no room

for mourning

perplexed

time

swirls in circles

echoes

descend

nothing grows here

not even childhood

breath

poised on the edge

the shadow   abandoned

yet again

misplaced

slice of moon

at daybreak

beginning to drown

uncertain

time

running racing

blackened

mirror

incapable

of reflection

time

gathered

dust

exiled moon

awaiting the morning

lingers

gather

autumn leaves

abandon

all thought

of another spring

her eyes

trace

the passing of time

slate grey

pool of memory

the stone

sinking in eyes

grown shadowless

an earlier self

dreaming a poem

foretelling

its own death

silent

echo

running through

huddled leaves

groping for words

simmer

sheer white

eyes filled

with night

shadows

in a heap

broken time

after time

somewhere a clock

keeping *what else*

time

camouflaged dawn

upside down

emptied drop

by drop

eyes

shut tight

feign sleep

the night wears

a dream

steals past

the words

between lines

trapped time

another winter

stifles whispers

of a fresh spring

in tatters

the night

stench of burnt time

crushed time

time underfoot

words crawl home

to die

blind shadows

run out of time

seek another shelter

rush

night

move

move

bitter dawn

lament your own death

draw blood

stab the dark

blind

death deposited

at my doorstep

thick

with the smell of yesterday's love

no room now

for light to linger

a spider's tongue crawls

fills the page

white shroud

digging

    words

    forgotten over time

memory   buried

in its grave

    half-formed words

stolen

from time

    heavy-footed

tongue dragging its feet

    breathless

stay a little longer

I whispered too late

in her arms

she cradled

newborn shadows

alone

outside the window

begging to be let in

the night

the sun

laments its own drowning

forsaken debris

of a memory

coiled

wisp of smoke

winter candle

light

flicker

die

rain tremble

behind eyelids

twilight

grey

forlorn

the clouds

        the stillness of the night

the wind full of

rumours of an early dawn

        come to grieve

the autumn leaf

as it falls

                falls

to the ground

her

eyes

dark with night

filled   brimming over

a deserted look

the dream

                                        flees

shivers

runs through

the earth

time

wounded

sinks to the ground

losing

its way

the dark

continues to whisper

in its sleep

smoke

from

a burnt-out candle

runs

through the air

like passing desire

cold grey

reticent dusk

like premonition

a stirring among the shadows

anticipates

the dark

night made white

by snow

time

stands trembling

shadows dazzled

by the blinding light

confused

circle overhead

raven

time

shatters

  ghostlike

the night

descends

  on a bed of frost

white

slipping

into the grey

abandoned time

out of breath

wanders

by night

by day

MOTHER MUSE V

how would I guess that you slept with your eyes open
and your mouth too I believe you did
later we found roughly sharpened pencils
blue red black under your pillow their fresh shavings
in your rubber slippers beside the bed but no blade
writing the night copying poems from memory
growing up in a small town run by a motor-car company
you lose your way in thoughts while waiting for the ashes
to cool I read the sign on the green plastic trash can that says
'no hot liquids and ashes allowed'

been a while since I saw the moon at dawn
but it is known to happen

that spider web
you brush
from your eyes
flicking fears
smashing them
against the plaster
in frustration
at how things came to pass
that morning made helpless
you backtrack rewind

a bit   *just*   that tiny bit

and you listen
all over again   you listen
to her asking for tea

endings
endings *unending*
night   *how you grow pale*

breathe into   this parting
punctuated
by urgency

I would *if I could night*   sing you awake
among the   birdcall
the   barking of dogs

a sky   (there being many)
contemplates
its vast nothingness
and then
decisively
shuts out the thought

clouds folded over
and over again

and to think that   the book of life

has both running heads and
running feet
in equal measure

inherit night
            fate

toothless   string
trailing

float
kite
without moorings

crows gnaw
at your pink   your blue
your yellow

trailing
trailing

Ten silver prints

I close my eyes against the glare of the sun.

I follow the path of the rainbow.

It takes me to the pool of water.

Beneath the surface of the mirror.

Tiny eddies bearing reflections.

Light gathered from the sun.

A stillness that is as restless as it is quiet.

I take off my shadow and watch it drown.

Somewhere in the distance.

A church bell strikes twelve.

this shadow   its plaster face peeling
hanging
          upside down
from a ceiling

over   a bed
                    that reverberates
each time the local train
passes overhead

sits a   woman

her shadow   refuses   to hurl itself
out of the window

are you there somewhere there. where my words may.
just may. reach you. among thoughts. that loiter. refusing
to bestir. rustle turn twist shake themselves. awake. out.
of the numbness. or stupor. they find themselves
enveloped in. or by. our yesterdays. staleness refusing. to
leave. stench palpable. the dead had. tenanted the place.
choke the tears. out of eyes. already red from. lack. of
sleep. the need to stay. alert. stay awake. keep dreams at
bay. distanced. fenced out. or in. remain out of reach.
matter. of putting one's hand. firmly on head. pushing.
hard downwards. keep the pressure. stifle struggle.
deliberate drowned. perhaps not. like something. that did
not. take place happen. except maybe. imagined or just.

fancied.

The leaves gathered their whispers. First into a murmur. Then into a song.

Dance, *dance*
this
one
last
time
wisp of smoke

fragile piece
of silver hanging
by a thread
in the light of dawn

climb down
pale moon

as it moved the light stood still moving
with purpose between the tree and the tree
in a motion less ness between the tree
and the tree the light stood moving
with purpose into the shade

elsewhere

stripped of shadow the light
stilled elsewhere the discarded
shadows gather conspiring autumn
leaves conjuring

conjuring
the possibility of a storm

For John Ashbery

shut the door slam
it shut the door shut
it slam it the door

it's memory's turn to find its way
through the house that
is no longer yours to explore

and the wind
the wind needs to know
which way to blow

shut the door
slam
it shut
the door
shut it
slam it

burn the incense bury
the gold begin
the process of anointing

yourself

rather than wait
for the angel in black
to do the work for you

a god lying in wait
for a death foretold
at birth

oblivious grave   catch
            time as it ages
your breath
coming in short spurts
as you row against the wind
            upstream
bury the twilight
in your fist full of sand
from a breathless hourglass
hear
            the murmur
of your last dream   remember
there are no more straws
only a pale moon   and
the anticipation
of an unexpected dawn

shavings from a pencil sharpen razor blade cut into finger
lines chisel lead rough then smooth rotate wheel spin till a
degree of perfection is achieved

now stab each palm between the eyes then spread five
fingers then ten then make the most of your pain all the
while trying to remember if there is an afterlife

curious that you run naked against the crowds looking
right through you unfazed even blank eyes wide open
unafraid of your bloodied footprints on the snow

remember that losing one's memory is no longer
something that happens to other people
you forget slowly you need help to put the shards together

the cracks in the mirror widening the jigsaw no longer
resembles the image on the table what table you ask
what image what mirror

you know already that the lucid is not always the fog
it is often made out to be as you crush crystals beneath
your feet

all the while seeking the crumbs you left strewn around
from an earlier memory game a slope made hesitant as
you climb

opaque
frosted over
with our breath
no longer fresh

winter

giving way
to
bitterspring

Like a prayer
I folded your hand into mine.

diningtable white
marble with flawed streaks
blackpatches turned grey into
yellow from countless spillings of tea
and such like or peeledfruits
their juices rivuletting
like foreseeable futures
we didn't begbargain for
as the house she left behind
slipslipping its moorings
adriftrudderless sailing
away into a storm

each step a bent despair
your striding a hurried silhouette
the cloud above your head
a figment of light
the sky a camouflage
of abandoned vapour
offering
no rain
                no reason
                                no consolation

[*bitter*
parting
bitter parting]

I find my way into the fog

by way of the dream that gags my footsteps with shadows
recruited for this very purpose

the light does a quick math as it reduces the night
to half

the moon loosens its rope and slips out of its skin walking
naked into the fog by way of my dream one hand pressing
down on the shadow as it gags all sound thereby reducing
all resistance into abrupt silence

elsewhere a river in turbulence gnashes its teeth smashes
its head into the rocks while the light adept at swift calcu-
lations minuses the shadow from the light ties the loose
ends left behind by the hurriedly departing dream the one
that had gagged my footsteps with shadows the ones that
had been recruited for this very purpose

I look for a match to light myself into a ball of fire the
flames emitting a crackling sound

I lose my way into the fog

One morning I woke up and found that the mirror no longer reflected my face

A light in the distance.
Steady. Unwavering flame.
It's footsteps in tune.
With the whispering snow.

I reached for my old lamp. Frosted over.
Cracked with the cold. Wiped it clean.
Striking a match. I coaxed the light out of it.

Then I hung it on the door.

In case you needed to find your way home.

The conversations around you. Brittle and brisk. Without meaning. Words hurriedly strung together. Shoved into a tin can. Shaken. Made to rattle in short bursts. Like gunfire at close quarters. Tweets of fate. And happenstance. Like firing squads. Immediate. Transient. Relentless and vicarious babel. Grab and shoot. Who has the time? To think? Or breathe. The normal? Now a different shade of pale. Like running a hundred-metre dash in less than nine seconds. On shards of glass. Breathless. And bleeding. Gladiator sport. The kind that seeks out language only to thrust a sword into it. While the mob brays. For more bloodletting.

Slow everything down. Let your fingers grind to a halt. The forty-five on your turntable. Your skin scraping the grooves. Slurring the song. As if strangling the words. Almost.

Start afresh. Begin a new sentence. A long one. One in which with extreme patience and a strong dose of diligence you once again lay down the ground rules for language with a past history of elegance and a turn of phrase that makes you gasp with admiration for the one who has penned it with such élan and taste and wit and a sense of literary tradition passed on from writer to writer through centuries of fine writing where the meaning of words as they combine and mingle with each other takes precedence over mere ornamentation and where the complexity and density of a thought is chiselled to succinct and purposeful perfection in a heady mixture of fine prose or poetry or drama or whatever be your particular calling.

Now punctuate it.

For John Ashbery

unfamiliar this silence stuck in a throat used to giving voice
to the *important* and the *momentous*

is this speechlessness 'unable to say the *familiar* things'?

Leaving behind a desolate shadow
her body left home in silence

ALSO FROM SPEAKING TIGER

KNOTTED GRIEF

Naveen Kishore

'Form and content come together beautifully in Naveen Kishore's haiku-like poems about loss and desolation.'—*The Hindu*

In his first book of poems, renowned publisher Naveen Kishore shows us—without holding back, and yet with compassion—grief, deep and bewildering; cruelties, public and private. He lays bare the nature of our outer and inner realities, using striking symbolism to reveal what humans are capable of doing to each other. The early part of the collection, 'Kashmiriyat', is a visceral monument to shadows, widows and unlived lives, constructed with one hundred and five stanzas. In the 'Selected Griefs' that follow, the wounds are intimate, everyday, but the images remind us of the world's brutalities—and what, then, is innocent? By depicting large-scale human tragedies and familiar habits and hurts within the same covers, the poet tests himself, and us.

'So why do we read about grief and sit with our sadness when the world around us is already on fire? *Knotted Grief* reminds us that our sorrow can also be our life source—it can teach us to create, value, fight and resist, and ultimately, find joy in living.'—Scroll.in